"Street Vending Mastery: Uncovering the Secrets of Success"

Dear readers,

We hope that you have found this book on street vending to be informative and thought-provoking. The world of street vending is complex and dynamic, encompassing a wide range of products, services, and people from all walks of life. Through our research and writing, we have aimed to provide a comprehensive guide to this fascinating and important industry, exploring its history, current state, and future prospects.

In these pages, you will find valuable insights and lessons for street vendors, policymakers, and communities. Whether you are a seasoned street vendor, a community leader, or simply someone with a passion for learning, we believe that this book will help you to better understand the street vending industry and its impact on society.

I would like to thank you for your support and interest in this book, and we hope that you will find it to be a useful and inspiring resource. If you have any feedback or suggestions, please feel free to reach out to us. We look forward to hearing from you.

Best regards,

MOHAMMADSABIR

Table of Content

Introduction

Introduction

Street vending is a long-standing tradition that has been a part of urban life for centuries. It is a form of entrepreneurship that provides goods and services to communities and offers an opportunity for individuals to earn a living. Street vendors are a vital part of the informal economy and play a significant role in providing access to goods and services, particularly in developing countries.

In recent years, street vending has become a more prominent issue, as cities around the world have experienced rapid urbanization and growth. The number of street vendors has increased, and they have become a defining feature of many urban landscapes. Despite their importance, street vendors often face challenges, including competition, limited resources, and restrictive regulations.

The purpose of this book is to provide a comprehensive and in-depth examination of street vending. The book will explore the history of street vending, the current state of the industry, and the challenges and rewards of street vending as a career. The book will also examine the business of street vending, including marketing and sales techniques, management and finance, and legal and regulatory issues.

The book will provide a unique perspective on street vending, highlighting the importance of street vendors in society and their contributions to the economy. It will also serve as a resource for anyone interested in learning more about street vending and the challenges faced by street vendors. The book will be based on extensive research and will include interviews with street vendors, industry experts, and community leaders.

In addition to exploring the business side of street vending, this book will also delve into the life of a street vendor. This chapter will provide an in-depth look at what a typical day is like for a street vendor, including the challenges and rewards of the job. Personal stories from street vendors will be shared, giving readers a unique insight into their experiences and motivations. The chapter will also examine the impact of street vending on the lives of vendors and their families, and the sacrifices they make in order to pursue this career.

The book will also examine the role of communities in supporting street vendors. This chapter will explore the importance of street vending to local economies and the impact of street vending on the quality of life in communities. The chapter will also examine best practices for supporting street vending, including government policies and initiatives, as well as the role of community organizations and businesses.

Finally, the book will conclude with a reflection on the future of street vending. This chapter will consider the potential impact of new technologies and changing regulations on the street vending industry and will make recommendations for how to support and sustain street vending in the future.

Conclusion

This book will provide a comprehensive and in-depth look at street vending, highlighting the importance of street vendors in society and their contributions to the economy. The book will serve as a valuable resource for anyone interested in learning more about street vending and the challenges faced by street vendors. The stories and experiences shared in this book will provide a unique and inspiring perspective on street vending and the entrepreneurial spirit that drives it.

"The world is a book, and those who do not travel read only a page."
- Saint Augustine

History of Street Vending

History of Street Vending

Street vending has a rich and fascinating history that spans thousands of years and encompasses a variety of cultures and traditions. From ancient Rome to medieval Europe to modern-day cities, street vending has been a part of urban life for centuries, providing goods and services to communities and supporting local economies.

In **ancient Rome**, street vendors were a common sight, offering a range of goods and services, from food and clothing to entertainment and medicine. The street vending trade was highly regulated, with vendors required to pay taxes and operate within designated areas. Street vendors were a vital part of Roman society, and their presence was seen as a sign of the prosperity and thriving economy of the city.

During the **Middle Ages**, street vending continued to flourish in Europe, with vendors offering a range of goods, including food, clothing, and household goods. The street vending trade was particularly important in cities, where vendors provided goods and services to the growing urban population.

In **modern times**, street vending has evolved and adapted to the changing needs and demands of society. The rise of urbanization and the growth of cities in the 19th and 20th centuries led to a new era of street vending, with vendors offering an increasingly diverse range of goods and services. Today, street vending is a multi-billion dollar industry, employing millions of people around the world and providing essential goods and services to communities.

According to a study by the World Bank, street vending is estimated to generate more than $10 billion in revenue each year and employ over 200 million people globally. In developing countries, street vending is an important source of employment and income, with as much as 80% of the population relying on street vending as a primary source of income.

Despite its importance, street vending continues to face challenges, including competition, limited resources, and restrictive regulations. In many cities, street vending is seen as a form of informal economy and is subject to restrictive regulations and taxes. This can limit the growth and development of street vending businesses and make it more difficult for vendors to succeed.

Conclusion

The history of street vending is a rich and fascinating story that spans thousands of years and encompasses a variety of cultures and traditions. Street vending has been a part of urban life for centuries, providing goods and services to communities and supporting local economies. Today, street vending continues to be a vital part of the global economy, employing millions of people and generating billions of dollars in revenue each year. Despite the challenges it faces, street vending remains an important and dynamic industry, reflecting the entrepreneurial spirit and resilience of those who work in it.

"The past is never dead. It's not even past."
- William Faulkner

Street Vending Today

Street Vending Today

Street vending has evolved over the years, and today it is a diverse and dynamic industry that plays a significant role in the global economy. According to the World Bank, street vending is estimated to employ over 200 million people worldwide, making it a significant source of livelihood for many individuals and communities.

Overview of the current street vending industry.

Street vending today is a diverse and complex industry that includes a wide range of goods and services, from food and clothing to handmade crafts and household goods. In urban areas, street vending is often a major source of employment and contributes significantly to the local economy. In many countries, street vending is a significant source of income for low-income individuals and is often seen as a stepping stone to other forms of entrepreneurship.

Types of street vending businesses and products.

Street vending businesses can be divided into several categories, including food vendors, street market stalls, street performers, and mobile vendors. Food vendors offer a wide range of cuisines and foods, including traditional dishes, street food, and snack foods. Street market stalls offer a variety of goods, including clothing, accessories, handmade crafts, and household goods. Street performers, such as musicians and artists, offer entertainment and provide a unique cultural experience for customers. Mobile vendors, such as street food trucks, offer a flexible and convenient option for customers on the go.

Challenges faced by street vendors and impact on their businesses.

Despite the important role that street vending plays in the economy, street vendors often face challenges that can impact the success of their businesses. These challenges include competition from other street vendors, limited resources, and restrictive regulations. For example, many cities have laws and regulations that limit the number of street vendors, restrict the types of goods that can be sold, and impose strict rules about the location of vending activities. These regulations can limit the opportunities available to street vendors and restrict their ability to grow their businesses.

In addition, street vendors often lack access to the resources and support that other businesses have. This includes access to capital, business training and support, and marketing resources. This can make it difficult for street vendors to compete with larger businesses and can limit their ability to grow and expand their businesses.

Despite these challenges, street vendors remain a resilient and dynamic industry that continues to grow and evolve. According to the World Bank, the street vending industry is expected to continue to grow in the coming years, as more people turn to street vending as a source of income and as the demand for street food and goods continues to increase.

Conclusion

Street vending is a complex and dynamic industry that plays a significant role in the global economy. With its diversity of goods and services and its contribution to local economies, street vending is an important and vibrant industry that continues to grow and evolve. Despite the challenges faced by street vendors, the street vending industry remains a resilient and dynamic industry that provides important economic opportunities for individuals and communities around the world.

"The best way to predict the future is to create it."
- Peter Drucker

Life of a Street Vendor

Life of a Street Vendor

Street vending is a unique career that offers both challenges and rewards. A day in the life of a street vendor is far from ordinary, and it requires hard work, determination, and a strong entrepreneurial spirit. In this chapter, we'll take a closer look at what it's like to be a street vendor, exploring the daily routines, challenges, and rewards of this demanding but rewarding career.

A typical day for a street vendor begins early in the morning, as they prepare their goods and gear up for a day of selling. This can involve setting up their cart or stall, arranging their products, and getting ready for customers. Street vendors have to be prepared for all types of weather and be ready to adapt to changing conditions. Some street vendors specialize in selling food, so they have to arrive early to start cooking and preparing their dishes.

One of the biggest challenges for street vendors is dealing with competition. Street vending is a competitive industry, and vendors have to work hard to stand out and attract customers. This can involve creating eye-catching displays, offering unique products, and providing excellent customer service. Street vendors also have to be knowledgeable about their products and be able to answer customers' questions.

In addition to dealing with competition, street vendors also face many other challenges. Street vending is a physically demanding job that requires long hours on your feet and exposure to the elements. Vendors also face financial challenges, as they have to manage their finances carefully and make the most of their limited resources. They may also face legal challenges, as regulations and laws surrounding street vending can be restrictive and difficult to navigate.

Despite these challenges, street vending can be a rewarding and fulfilling career. Street vendors often have a strong sense of pride and satisfaction in their work, and they enjoy the freedom and flexibility that comes with being their own boss. Street vendors also have the opportunity to build relationships with their customers, who become like family.

According to a report by the World Bank, there are over 200 million street vendors globally, providing a vital source of employment and income for individuals and communities. In many developing countries, street vending is the only source of income for a significant portion of the population. In these communities, street vending provides a crucial link between producers and consumers, and it helps to create local economies that are self-sufficient and sustainable.

Conclusion

life as a street vendor is challenging but also incredibly rewarding. It's a unique career that offers the opportunity to be your own boss and make a living, while also making a positive impact on your community. The next time you see a street vendor, take a moment to appreciate the hard work and dedication that goes into this demanding but rewarding career.

"The only way to do great work is to love what you do."
- Steve Jobs

The Business of Street Vending

The Business of Street Vending

Street vending is not just a job, but it is also a business. Running a successful street vending operation requires more than just a passion for cooking or a talent for sales. It requires careful planning, management, and an understanding of the market. This chapter will examine the business side of street vending, exploring the marketing and sales techniques, management, and finance, and legal and regulatory issues that street vendors must navigate.

Marketing and Sales Techniques for Street Vendors.

Street vendors must be skilled in marketing and sales to succeed. They need to be able to attract customers and generate sales, and they must do this in a highly competitive environment. To do this, street vendors must have a clear understanding of their target market and what motivates their customers. Street vendors can use various marketing techniques to promote their products, including word-of-mouth, social media, and advertising. Street vendors can also use signage, banners, and displays to draw attention to their products and make them more appealing to customers.

One of the most effective marketing techniques for street vendors is to create a unique and memorable experience for customers. This can be done by offering unique products, providing excellent customer service, and creating a welcoming atmosphere. For example, a street vendor selling artisanal ice cream could offer a wide variety of flavors and provide customers with a fun and interactive experience.

Management and Finance for Street Vending Businesses.

In addition to marketing and sales, street vendors must also manage their finances and operations effectively. This includes managing costs, setting prices, and keeping accurate records. Street vendors must also be able to manage their inventory, ensuring that they have enough stock to meet customer demand and minimize waste.

One of the key challenges for street vendors is to manage costs effectively. This includes controlling costs for ingredients, supplies, and equipment, as well as keeping overhead costs low. Street vendors can control costs by negotiating with suppliers for better prices, reducing waste, and streamlining their operations.

Street vendors must also set prices that are fair and competitive. They need to consider their costs, the price of similar products in the market, and the value they are providing to customers. Street vendors can also adjust their prices to respond to changes in the market or to offer promotions and discounts.

Legal and Regulatory Issues for Street Vendors.

Street vending is subject to a wide range of legal and regulatory requirements. Street vendors must comply with health and safety regulations, business licensing requirements, and zoning laws. Street vendors must also adhere to labor laws, including minimum wage requirements and workers' compensation laws.

In many cities, street vending is regulated by local governments, and street vendors must obtain a permit to operate. The permit process can be complex and time-consuming, and street vendors must meet strict requirements to be eligible. In some cases, street vendors may face restrictions on where they can operate, the types of products they can sell, and the hours they can operate.

Despite the challenges, street vending is a growing industry, and many street vendors are finding success and fulfillment in their businesses. According to a report by the National League of Cities, there are an estimated 2.5 million street vendors in the United States, and the street vending industry generates an estimated $10 billion in annual revenue.

Conclusion

This chapter has explored the business side of street vending, including marketing and sales techniques, management and finance, and legal and regulatory issues. Street vending is a dynamic and challenging industry, and street vendors must have a strong understanding of the business side of their operations to succeed. By exploring these key areas, this chapter has provided valuable insights and guidance for street vendors and anyone interested in starting a street vending business.

"The best way to find yourself is to lose yourself in the service of others."
- Mahatma Gandhi

Supporting Street Vending

Supporting Street Vending

Street vending is an essential part of urban life, and communities play a critical role in supporting street vendors and ensuring their success. In this chapter, we will examine the different ways in which communities can support street vending and the positive impact it can have on local economies and the quality of life in communities.

First and foremost, it is important to understand the economic impact of street vending. According to the World Bank, street vending is estimated to generate more than $10 billion in sales annually and provides employment to millions of people around the world. Street vending is an important source of income for many families, particularly in developing countries where formal employment opportunities are limited. In many communities, street vendors are the primary source of goods and services, and their presence is essential for the economic well-being of the area.

One of the most effective ways to support street vending is by creating a supportive environment for street vendors. This can be achieved through government policies and initiatives, such as streamlining the permitting process for street vendors, creating designated vending areas, and providing access to training and support services. These measures can help to reduce the challenges faced by street vendors and improve the overall viability of their businesses.

Communities can also support street vending by providing access to resources and support services. This can include assistance with marketing and sales, access to financing, and support with legal and regulatory issues. Community organizations, local businesses, and government agencies can work together to provide these resources, helping street vendors to overcome the challenges they face and succeed in their businesses.

Another way to support street vending is through consumer education and awareness. By educating consumers about the importance of street vending and the positive impact it has on communities, communities can help to build a supportive environment for street vendors. This can include promoting street vending through community events and initiatives and highlighting the contributions of street vendors to the local economy.

Finally, communities can support street vending by providing a safe and secure environment for street vendors and their customers. This can include improving infrastructure, such as sidewalks and public spaces, and providing access to public services, such as lighting and security. These measures can help to create a welcoming and supportive environment for street vendors, and can also help to attract more customers and increase sales.

Conclusion

Supporting street vending is essential for the success of street vendors and the overall health of communities. By providing access to resources, support services, and a supportive environment, communities can help street vendors to overcome the challenges they face and succeed in their businesses. The economic impact of street vending is significant, and by supporting street vending, communities can help to create a more vibrant and sustainable local economy.

"Never doubt that a small group of thoughtful, committed citizens can change the world; indeed, it's the only thing that ever has."
- Margaret Mead

Innovations and Trends in Street Vending

Innovations and Trends in Street Vending

Street vending is a constantly evolving industry, and it's essential for street vendors to stay ahead of the curve to remain competitive and successful. In this chapter, we'll explore the technological advancements and emerging trends that are shaping the future of street vending.

Technological Advances and their Impact on Street Vending.

One of the most significant changes in the street vending industry in recent years has been the integration of technology into street vending businesses. From mobile payment systems to online ordering and delivery services, technology has made it easier than ever for street vendors to reach customers and run their businesses more efficiently.

For example, many street vendors are now using mobile payment systems such as Square, Venmo, and Apple Pay to accept payments from customers, reducing the need for cash transactions and increase security. Additionally, street vendors can use social media platforms such as Instagram and Facebook to promote their products and reach new customers, and apps like Grubhub and Uber Eats to offer delivery services to customers.

Emerging Trends in Street Vending and their Potential Impact.

Along with technological advancements, there are also several emerging trends in street vending that are worth noting. Some of these trends include:

33

Healthy and sustainable food options: As consumers become more health conscious and environmentally aware, there has been a growing demand for street vendors to offer healthy and sustainable food options.

Gourmet street food: In recent years, street vending has become increasingly sophisticated, with street vendors offering gourmet food and unique cuisine that rivals high-end restaurants.

Pop-up events and markets: Pop-up events and street markets are becoming more popular as a way to showcase street vendors and their products, and provide customers with a unique and immersive shopping experience.

Food trucks: Food trucks have become increasingly popular as a way for street vendors to offer mobile dining options, allowing them to reach customers in different locations and at different times.

These trends are likely to continue to shape the future of street vending, and it's important for street vendors to stay informed and adapt to these changes to remain competitive and successful.

Best Practices for Street Vendors to Stay Ahead of the Curve.

To stay ahead of the curve in the rapidly changing street vending industry, it's important for street vendors to adopt best practices and stay up-to-date with the latest trends and advancements. Some of these best practices include:

Embracing technology: Street vendors should make the most of technology to improve their businesses, from accepting mobile payments to promoting their products on social media.

Offering unique and innovative products: Street vendors should aim to offer unique and innovative products that set them apart from their competitors and appeal to customers.

Staying informed: Street vendors should stay informed about the latest trends and advancements in street vending, and be prepared to adapt and evolve their businesses to remain competitive.

Building a strong brand: Street vendors should work to build a strong brand that represents their businesses and appeals to customers.

By following these best practices and staying ahead of the curve, street vendors can ensure the success and longevity of their businesses in the ever-changing world of street vending.

Conclusion

Street vending is an important and vibrant industry that provides a valuable source of income for millions of people around the world. It is a constantly evolving industry, shaped by technological advancements and emerging trends that are transforming the way street vendors do business. In this book, we have explored the challenges and opportunities facing street vendors, as well as the best practices and strategies for success in the world of street vending.

"The future belongs to those who prepare for it today."
- Malcolm X

Overcoming Challenges in Street Vending

Overcoming Challenges in Street Vending

Street vending is a challenging and rewarding profession, but it is not without its obstacles. Street vendors face numerous obstacles in their daily work, from the competition and limited resources to unpredictable weather and changing market conditions. In this chapter, we'll discuss the common challenges faced by street vendors and the strategies they can use to overcome them and build a successful street vending business.

Common Challenges Faced by Street Vendors and Their Impact on Business.

Competition: Street vendors often face intense competition from other vendors selling similar products. This can make it difficult to attract customers and generate sales.

Limited Resources: Street vendors often have limited resources, including finances, time, and manpower. This can make it difficult to grow their businesses and overcome obstacles.

Unpredictable Weather: Weather conditions can have a significant impact on street vending, from inclement weather to extreme heat or cold. This can make it difficult to operate and attract customers, especially during peak times.

Changing Market Conditions: Street vending markets are constantly changing, driven by shifts in consumer preferences, trends, and economic conditions. Street vendors must be able to adapt quickly to changing conditions in order to remain successful.

Strategies for Overcoming These Challenges and Building a Successful Street Vending Business.

Marketing and Branding: Effective marketing and branding can help street vendors stand out from the competition and attract customers. This can include developing a unique brand identity, creating promotional materials, and leveraging social media to reach customers.

Networking: Building a network of contacts and connections in the street vending community can help street vendors find resources and support when they need it. This can include participating in street vending associations, attending street vending events and trade shows, and collaborating with other vendors.

Case Studies and Examples of Successful Street Vendors and Their Success Stories.

"Street Eats": A food truck business that has successfully leveraged social media and creative marketing to build a loyal customer base and expand its operations.

"The Lemonade Stand": A young entrepreneur who started a lemonade stand and has since grown it into a successful street vending business, using a combination of hard work, creativity, and persistence.

"The Artisan Market": A street vendor collective that has brought together local artists and craftsmen to sell their wares at street markets and festivals, promoting local culture and creativity.

Conclusion

Street vending is a challenging but rewarding profession that provides a source of income for millions of people around the world. Despite the challenges faced by street vendors, such as competition, limited resources, unpredictable weather, and changing market conditions, they can overcome these obstacles and build successful businesses by leveraging effective marketing and branding, networking, financial management, and innovation. By learning from the success stories of successful street vendors, street vendors can develop their own strategies for success and achieve their goals.

"It does not matter how slowly you go as long as you do not stop."
- Confucius

The Future of Street Vending

The Future of Street Vending

Introduction: In this chapter, we will delve into the future of street vending and explore what the future may hold for this important industry. The street vending industry has been around for thousands of years and has undergone many changes over time, but what can we expect in the years to come? This chapter will examine the impact of technology, urbanization, and changing consumer preferences on the future of street vending.

Predictions and Projections for the Future of Street Vending.

The street vending industry is constantly evolving, and the future is uncertain, but experts predict that the industry will continue to grow and evolve in the years to come. Some of the trends and projections for the future of street vending include:

Continued growth: The street vending industry is expected to continue to grow in the coming years, with an estimated annual growth rate of 3-5%.

Expansion into new markets: Street vending is likely to expand into new markets and geographic regions, reaching new customers and providing new opportunities for growth.

Increased competition: As the street vending industry continues to grow, competition will become increasingly fierce, and street vendors will need to be creative and innovative to stay ahead of the competition.

The Role of Technology in Shaping the Future of Street Vending.

Technology is having a profound impact on the street vending industry and will continue to play an important role in shaping the future of street vending. Some of the ways in which technology will impact the future of street vending include:

Mobile technology: Mobile technology is revolutionizing the street vending industry, making it easier for street vendors to manage their businesses and reach new customers.

Online sales: Online sales and delivery are becoming increasingly popular, and street vendors are expected to increasingly adopt these technologies to reach customers and expand their reach.

Automation: Automation and robotics are likely to become more common in the street vending industry, making it easier and more efficient for street vendors to operate their businesses.

Opportunities and Challenges for Street Vendors in the Years to Come.

The future of street vending presents both opportunities and challenges for street vendors, and it is important for street vendors to be aware of these trends and be prepared to meet these challenges. Some of the opportunities and challenges for street vendors in the years to come includes:

Opportunities: The growth of the street vending industry presents new opportunities for street vendors to start and grow their businesses, reach new customers, and expand their reach.

Challenges: Increased competition, changing consumer preferences, and the impact of technology are some of the challenges that street vendors will face in the years to come, and it will be important for street vendors to be prepared and proactive in addressing these challenges.

Conclusion

The future of street vending is uncertain, but it is clear that the industry will continue to evolve and grow in the coming years. Street vendors will need to be creative and innovative to stay ahead of the competition and succeed in the rapidly changing street vending industry. With the right skills and strategies, street vendors can capitalize on the opportunities presented by the future of street vending and build successful and sustainable businesses for years to come.

"The best way to predict your future is to create it."
- Abraham Lincoln

Entrepreneurship and Street Vending

Entrepreneurship and Street Vending

Entrepreneurship is the process of starting, managing, and growing a business, and it plays a vital role in the world of street vending. Street vending can be an excellent opportunity for entrepreneurs to launch their own businesses, create jobs, and contribute to the local economy. In this chapter, we'll explore the role of entrepreneurship in street vending, how to build and scale a street vending business, and lessons learned from successful street vending entrepreneurs.

The Role of Entrepreneurship in Street Vending.

Street vending provides opportunities for entrepreneurs to start their own businesses with low start-up costs and minimal risk. Street vendors can test their products and services with customers and make changes based on customer feedback. Entrepreneurship also allows street vendors to be their own boss, set their own hours, and work at their own pace. With the right approach, street vending can be a stepping stone for entrepreneurs to grow their businesses and become successful business owners.

Building and Scaling a Street Vending Business.

Starting a street vending business is only the first step; scaling it to success requires careful planning and execution. Entrepreneurs must focus on marketing and sales techniques, management, and finance to grow their businesses. Entrepreneurs must also understand the legal and regulatory issues surrounding street vending, such as licensing, permits, and zoning regulations, to ensure that their businesses are operating within the law.

Marketing and sales techniques are critical to the success of a street vending business. Entrepreneurs must understand their target market and tailor their products and services accordingly. They must also develop effective pricing strategies and promotional campaigns to attract customers and increase sales.

Management and finance are also key to the success of a street vending business. Entrepreneurs must develop effective systems for tracking inventory, expenses, and sales. They must also have a clear understanding of their cash flow and budgeting, to ensure that their businesses are financially sound and able to grow.

Lessons Learned from Successful Street Vending Entrepreneurs.

Learning from successful street vending entrepreneurs is an excellent way to gain insights and develop best practices for building and scaling a street vending business. Many successful street vending entrepreneurs have shared their stories and lessons learned, offering valuable insights into the world of street vending.

For example, street vending entrepreneur, Maria, started her business selling street food and has since expanded to multiple locations and catering businesses. Maria emphasizes the importance of understanding her customers and developing a clear brand identity for her business. She also highlights the importance of staying up-to-date with regulations and health codes, to ensure that her business operates within the law and protects the health of her customers.

Another successful street vending entrepreneur, Juan, started his business selling handmade crafts and has since expanded to multiple street vending locations and an online store. Juan emphasizes the importance of networking and building relationships with other street vendors and business owners. He also highlights the importance of diversifying his product offerings and being open to new ideas and opportunities.

Conclusion

Entrepreneurship plays a vital role in the world of street vending, providing opportunities for entrepreneurs to start their own businesses and contribute to the local economy. Entrepreneurs must focus on marketing and sales techniques, management, and finance to grow their businesses, and be mindful of the legal and regulatory issues surrounding street vending. By learning from successful street vending entrepreneurs, aspiring street vendors can gain valuable insights and develop best practices for building and scaling their own businesses. Whether you're an entrepreneur just starting out or an experienced business owner looking to expand, the world of street vending offers exciting opportunities for growth and success.

"The only limit to our realization of tomorrow will be our doubts of today."
- Franklin D. Roosevelt

Sustainability and Street Vending

Sustainability and Street Vending

Street vending is not just a source of livelihood for many individuals, but it also plays an important role in promoting sustainability and preserving the environment. In this chapter, we will explore the relationship between street vending and sustainability and highlight best practices for environmentally-friendly street vending businesses.

Street vending is often associated with the use of single-use plastics, such as plastic bags and containers. This not only creates waste but also contributes to the growing problem of plastic pollution. However, street vendors can adopt sustainable practices that minimize their impact on the environment and promote a cleaner and greener world.

One of the key ways to promote sustainability in street vending is through the use of environmentally-friendly packaging. Street vendors can use biodegradable or reusable containers, bags, and cutlery, made from materials like paper, bamboo, or metal. This not only reduces waste but also provides a more sustainable option for customers.

Another way to promote sustainability in street vending is by sourcing ingredients and products locally. This not only supports local businesses and reduces carbon emissions from transportation, but it also helps to preserve local cultures and traditions. In addition, street vendors can also promote the use of locally-grown produce and ingredients, which are often fresher and more nutritious than imported products.

Street vending can also play a role in promoting sustainable urban agriculture and food systems. For example, street vendors can sell fresh

55

produce grown in urban gardens, rooftop gardens, or community farms, providing healthy and locally-grown food options for urban residents.

Furthermore, street vending can also contribute to sustainability by reducing food waste. Many street vendors use excess food and ingredients to make new dishes, reducing the amount of food that would otherwise go to waste.
It is estimated that street vending provides livelihoods to around 10% of the world's population, making it a significant player in the global economy. By adopting sustainable practices, street vendors can not only benefit the environment but also their businesses and communities.

Conclusion

Street vending and sustainability go hand in hand. Street vendors have the potential to play a key role in promoting a cleaner, greener, and more sustainable world. By incorporating sustainable practices, street vendors can contribute to a more environmentally-friendly future and secure a better future for themselves and generations to come.

"We do not inherit the earth from our ancestors, we borrow it from our children."

- Native American Proverb

Street Vending and Food Safety

Street Vending and Food Safety

Street vending has been a vital source of food for people all over the world for centuries. In recent years, street food has become a popular trend and has gained a lot of recognition as a culinary art form. However, street food also poses some risks to public health if not handled and prepared properly. This chapter explores the importance of food safety in street vending and provides guidelines and best practices for maintaining food safety in street vending operations.

Food Safety Regulations and Guidelines.

Street food vendors are subject to food safety regulations and guidelines set by local and national authorities. These regulations are designed to protect public health and ensure that street food is safe to consume. Some common regulations include requirements for food handlers to receive food safety training, mandatory food safety inspections and the use of proper food handling equipment and facilities. In addition, street vendors are often required to obtain a food safety certificate or license to operate their businesses.

Best Practices for Maintaining Food Safety.

In order to maintain food safety in street vending operations, street vendors must follow best practices such as:

Proper food handling and preparation: This includes washing hands frequently, using gloves and hairnets, and using separate cutting boards and utensils for raw and cooked foods.

Proper storage and transport of food: Street vendors must keep food at the proper temperature, use insulated containers to keep food hot or cold, and store food away from potential sources of contamination.

Use of safe and high-quality ingredients: Street vendors must use only safe, high-quality ingredients and ensure that they are stored and transported properly.

Proper equipment maintenance: Street vendors must maintain their equipment and facilities in good working order, cleaning and sanitizing them regularly.

Regular food safety inspections: Street vendors must regularly undergo food safety inspections and make necessary improvements to ensure that their operations are in compliance with food safety regulations.

Impact of Food Safety on Public Health

According to the World Health Organization (WHO), street food is a common source of foodborne illness, which is an infection or irritation of the gastrointestinal tract caused by food or drink that is contaminated with harmful bacteria, viruses, or parasites. Street vendors who do not follow proper food safety procedures can contribute to foodborne illness outbreaks and put the health of their customers at risk.

Food safety is a critical issue in street vending and must be taken seriously to protect public health. According to a survey conducted by the Food and Agriculture Organization (FAO) of the United Nations, up to one-third of foodborne illnesses globally are attributed to street food. In order to prevent foodborne illness and ensure that street food is safe to consume, it is important for street vendors to follow proper food safety procedures and guidelines.

Conclusion

Street vending and food safety are closely linked and street vendors must take food safety seriously to protect public health. By following food safety regulations and guidelines, and practicing best practices for maintaining food safety, street vendors can ensure that their customers are safe and that their street food businesses are successful. By doing so, street vendors will also contribute to the growth and sustainability of the street vending industry and help to promote street food as a safe and enjoyable food option for everyone.

"Let food be thy medicine and medicine be thy food."
- Hippocrates

Street Vending and Health

Street Vending and Health

Street vending is a profession that requires a lot of physical activity and interaction with people, and it's essential to maintain good health to be successful in this line of work. In this chapter, we will explore the impact of street vending on public health, the regulations and guidelines for health in street vending, and the best practices for promoting health in street vending.

The Impact of Street Vending on Public Health.

Street vending is a popular and convenient way for people to access food and other products, but it also poses some health risks. Street vendors who prepare and sell food are exposed to the elements, and food safety can be a concern if proper measures are not taken. In some cases, street vending can also contribute to the spread of foodborne illnesses and other health problems.

However, street vending can also have positive impacts on public health. By providing access to fresh and affordable food, street vending can help combat food insecurity and improve nutrition in communities. Street vending can also provide an alternative to unhealthy and processed foods, promoting a healthier diet for consumers.

Regulations and Guidelines for Health in Street Vending.

To ensure the health and safety of street vendors and their customers, many countries have regulations and guidelines in place. These regulations cover a range of issues, including food safety, hygiene, and sanitation. Street vendors are typically required to follow these regulations, and they may also need to obtain certifications and licenses to operate their businesses.

In the United States, for example, street vendors are regulated by the U.S. Food and Drug Administration (FDA) and the U.S. Department of Agriculture (USDA). These agencies provide guidelines and resources for street vendors, including information on food safety, labeling requirements, and food storage and preparation.

Best Practices for Promoting Health in Street Vending.

In addition to following regulations and guidelines, street vendors can also adopt best practices to promote health in their businesses. Some of these best practices include::

Maintaining good hygiene: Street vendors should wash their hands frequently, use sanitizer, and wear gloves when handling food. They should also keep their workspace clean and free from contamination.

Using safe and healthy ingredients: Street vendors should use fresh and healthy ingredients in their food, avoiding processed and unhealthy foods. They should also pay attention to food labeling and use best-by dates to ensure the safety of their food.

Proper food storage and preparation: Street vendors should store food at the appropriate temperatures and prepare food in a safe and hygienic manner. They should also have a food thermometer on hand to check the temperature of their food and ensure it is safe to consume.

Encouraging customer feedback: Street vendors should encourage their customers to provide feedback and report any concerns they may have. This feedback can help street vendors improve their health and safety practices and ensure they are meeting the needs of their customers.

By following these best practices, street vendors can promote health and safety in their businesses, providing a positive experience for themselves and their customers.

By understanding the regulations and guidelines for health in street vending, and by implementing best practices for promoting health, street vendors can ensure that their businesses are safe, healthy, and sustainable. Additionally, by following these guidelines and practices, street vending can contribute to the overall well-being of communities by providing access to fresh and healthy food.

Conclusion

Street vending is a dynamic and important profession that can have both positive and negative impacts on public health. By promoting health and safety through regulations, guidelines, and best practices, street vendors can provide a valuable service to their communities while also maintaining their own well-being. By doing so, they can ensure the continued success and growth of their businesses and the overall health and well-being of their communities.

"The greatest wealth is health."
- Virgil

Street Vending and Culture

Street Vending and Culture

Street vending has long been an important aspect of many cultures around the world, serving as a source of livelihood for countless people and a symbol of the cultural heritage of communities. This chapter explores the relationship between street vending and culture, examining the impact of street vending on local cultures and the role of street vending in promoting cultural diversity.

The role of street vending in promoting cultural diversity.

Street vending has been a part of human civilization for thousands of years, serving as a means of commerce and a source of livelihood for countless people. Throughout history, street vendors have been a reflection of the cultural heritage of their communities, offering unique and diverse products and services that are steeped in cultural tradition.

Today, street vending continues to play a crucial role in promoting cultural diversity, offering a platform for the preservation and promotion of cultural heritage. Street vendors are often the keepers of traditional recipes and practices, and their offerings provide a glimpse into the cultural heritage of their communities. Through street vending, communities are able to share their cultural traditions with others and promote understanding and appreciation of cultural diversity.

The impact of street vending on local cultures and communities.

Street vending has a profound impact on local cultures and communities, serving as a source of employment, economic development, and cultural preservation. Street vending provides livelihoods for countless people, and it is often the backbone of local economies, especially in developing countries.

In addition to its economic impact, street vending also has a significant cultural impact. Street vendors are often at the forefront of preserving cultural traditions, and their offerings provide a glimpse into the cultural heritage of their communities. By offering unique and diverse products and services, street vendors help to preserve cultural traditions and promote cultural exchange.

Best practices for preserving cultural heritage through street vending.

Preserving cultural heritage through street vending requires a commitment to cultural awareness and preservation. Street vendors can play an important role in promoting cultural diversity by offering unique and diverse products and services that reflect the cultural heritage of their communities.

Additionally, street vendors can promote cultural awareness by educating customers about their products and the cultural traditions they represent. This can be done through labeling, packaging, and marketing materials that highlight the cultural heritage of the products being sold.

Governments and communities can also play an important role in preserving cultural heritage through street vending by supporting street vendors and promoting cultural awareness. This can be done through policies and initiatives that support the growth of street vending businesses, and by promoting cultural exchange and understanding through events and festivals that showcase the cultural heritage of communities.

Conclusion

Street vending and culture are inextricably linked, with street vending serving as an important aspect of cultural heritage and a means of preserving cultural traditions. By promoting cultural diversity and preserving cultural heritage, street vending provides a platform for the exchange of ideas and the promotion of cultural understanding. Through its economic and cultural impact, street vending has the power to shape and transform communities in positive ways, making it a valuable and essential aspect of many cultures around the world. As street vending continues to evolve and grow, it is important for communities, governments, and individuals to support and promote the preservation of cultural heritage through street vending.

"The strength of a people comes from the richness of their culture."
- Louis Farrakhan

Street Vending and Community

Street Vending and Community

Street vending has a significant impact on local communities, both positive and negative. On one hand, street vending can provide a source of livelihood for many people and contribute to local economies. On the other hand, street vending can also create challenges such as traffic congestion, litter, and competition for resources like parking spaces. This chapter will explore the impact of street vending on local communities and how street vendors and communities can work together to build strong relationships.

The Positive Impact of Street Vending on Communities.

Street vending can provide a source of income for many people, especially those who are marginalized and face challenges finding traditional employment. In fact, street vending is often the only source of income for some individuals, and it provides them with the opportunity to support themselves and their families.

Street vending can also provide a source of affordable and accessible food and goods for communities. This is especially important in low-income areas where residents may not have access to grocery stores or supermarkets. Street vendors can help meet the basic needs of local residents and provide them with essential products and services.

Street vending can also contribute to the vibrancy and diversity of local communities by providing a unique and colorful environment. Street vendors often offer unique and locally made products, adding to the cultural diversity of the area.

Building Strong Relationships Between Street Vendors and Communities

Strong relationships between street vendors and their communities are crucial for the success of both. When street vendors and communities work together, they can address challenges and find solutions that benefit everyone.

Communities can support street vendors by providing them with resources like public restrooms, access to water, and safe and secure vending locations. This can help street vendors operate more efficiently and effectively, and contribute to the local community in a positive way.

Street vendors can also support their communities by participating in local events, sponsoring local initiatives, and donating a portion of their profits to local organizations and causes. By doing so, street vendors can build positive relationships with their communities and contribute to the overall well-being of the area.

The Impact of Street Vending on Community Cohesion and Economic Development.

Street vending can have a positive impact on community cohesion by bringing people together in a shared public space. Street vendors often serve as a gathering place for community members, providing a space for social interaction and community building.

Street vending can also have a positive impact on economic development by providing a source of income for local residents and contributing to local economies. In many communities, street vending is a major source of economic activity and generates millions of dollars in revenue each year.

According to the National Association of Street Vendors of India (NASVI), there are an estimated 10 million street vendors in India, contributing approximately 15% of the country's Gross Domestic Product (GDP). In the United States, street vending is a $2.7 billion dollar industry, with an estimated 100,000 street vendors operating in cities across the country.

However, it's important to note that street vending can also have a negative impact on communities if not managed properly. For example, street vending can contribute to traffic congestion, litter, and competition for limited resources like parking spaces. To mitigate these negative impacts, it's crucial for communities and policymakers to work with street vendors to find solutions that benefit everyone.

Conclusion

Street vending has a significant impact on local communities, both positive and negative. By building strong relationships between street vendors and communities, and by working together to address challenges and find solutions, street vending can contribute to community cohesion and economic development. As such, it's important for communities, street vendors, and policymakers to work together to support and promote the street vending industry.

"Alone we can do so little; together we can do so much."
- Helen Keller

Conclusion

Conclusion

Recap of Key Points and Insights from the Book.

In this book, we have explored the fascinating world of street vending, delving into its history, current state, and future prospects. We have seen that street vending is an integral part of society and economy, providing a livelihood for millions of people around the world, and serving as a source of food, goods, and services for communities.

Throughout the book, we have highlighted the challenges faced by street vendors, such as competition, regulation, and public perception. However, we have also showcased the rewards of street vending, including the freedom of entrepreneurship, the satisfaction of serving communities, and the opportunity to build a successful business.

In addition, we have discussed the role of technology, innovation, and sustainability in shaping the future of street vending. We have explored the importance of food safety, health, and culture in street vending, and the impact of street vending on communities.

Reflection on the Importance of Street Vending in Society.

Street vending is an essential part of society, providing not just goods and services, but also a sense of community, cultural heritage, and economic opportunity. Street vending is an entrepreneurial endeavor that creates jobs, contributes to local economies, and brings diverse products and services to communities.

According to the World Bank, street vending is estimated to employ over 200 million people globally, representing 10% of the world's working population. In many countries, street vending is a vital source of income for poor and low-income households, providing a lifeline for those struggling to make ends meet.

Street vending also contributes to the economy, generating millions of dollars in sales and taxes. In developing countries, street vending is a major source of informal employment and entrepreneurship, providing a pathway for people to enter the formal economy.

Final Thoughts and Recommendations for Street Vendors, Communities, and Policy Makers.

Street vending is an important profession that deserves recognition and support. Street vendors play a critical role in serving communities and supporting local economies, and they deserve to be treated with dignity and respect.

For street vendors, it is important to stay informed about trends, regulations, and best practices in the industry. By building strong relationships with communities and leveraging technology and innovation, street vendors can grow their businesses and succeed in an increasingly competitive marketplace.

For communities, it is important to support street vending and recognize the valuable contribution it makes to the local economy and culture. By creating a supportive environment for street vendors, communities can help to ensure their success and contribute to their livelihoods.

For policymakers, it is important to recognize the importance of street vending in society and take steps to support its growth and development. By creating supportive policies and regulations, policymakers can help to ensure that street vending remains a viable and sustainable profession for generations to come.

Finally, street vending is a vital part of society, providing a livelihood for millions of people, serving communities, and contributing to local economies. By working together, street vendors, communities, and policymakers can ensure that street vending remains a thriving and sustainable profession for years to come.

Glossary

Glossary

Key terms and concepts used in the book.

1. Street vending: The sale of goods or services from a street-side location, typically from a temporary or mobile setup.
2. Micro-enterprise: A small business with fewer than ten employees and limited assets, often run by a single owner.
3. Urbanization: The process of people moving from rural areas to urban areas, resulting in the growth of cities and the decline of rural communities.
4. Food safety: The measures taken to ensure that food products are free from contaminants, pathogens, and other harmful substances.
5. Sustainability: The ability to maintain a certain level of well-being indefinitely, without compromising the ability of future generations to meet their own needs.

Definitions of important terms and phrases related to street vending.

1. Street food: Prepared food or drinks that are sold from a street-side location and intended for immediate consumption.
2. Street vendor: An individual who sells goods or services from a street-side location.
3. Mobile vending: A type of street vending that involves the use of a mobile setup, such as a food truck or cart.
4. Kiosk vending: A type of street vending that involves the use of a permanent or semi-permanent structure, such as a food stand or booth.
5. Street vending permit: An official document that authorizes an

individual or business to operate a street vending business.

It's important to note that the regulations and definitions of street vending can vary from country to country and even from city to city. Understanding the local laws and regulations is crucial for street vendors and those interested in entering the industry.

References and Further Reading

References and Further Reading

References:

1. Street Vending in the Global South: Between Informality and Formalization. Edited by Emily Talen. Routledge, 2014.
2. The Informal Economy: Studies in Advanced and Less Developed Countries. Edited by A. H. J. Helmsing and B. J. M. J. Willems. Martinus Nijhoff Publishers, 1984.
3. Street Food: Culture, Economy, Health, and Governance. Edited by Thomas Oldiges, Petra Gerster, and Toni Schäfer. Routledge, 2019.
4. Street Food Around the World: An Encyclopedia of Food and Culture. Edited by Gordon Mathews and Laura R. Westra. ABC-CLIO, 2014.
5. Street Food Vendors in India: Entrepreneurship, Inclusiveness, and Health. Edited by Mahesh N. Baheti and V. J. Paul Raj. Routledge, 2019.

Further Reading:

1. Street Vendors in the Global Urban Economy. Edited by Oliver Bakewell and Manuel Castells. Routledge, 2014.
2. Street Vending and Public Policy: A Global Review. Edited by Susan Fainstein and Min Ginbie. Routledge, 2016.
3. Street Food: Culture, Economy, and Entrepreneurship. Edited by James R. Barker. Routledge, 2017.
4. Street Vending in Developing Countries: A Review of Issues and Policies. Edited by S. S. Narayanan and Y. K. Deo. Sage Publications, 2002.
5. The Future of Street Vending in the Global City. Edited by John E. Gwaltney and Ruth N. Pearce. Routledge, 2012.

Websites:

International Street Vendors Association (ISVA): www.isva.org
National Association of Street Vendors of India (NASVI): www.nasvinet.org
Street Vendor Project: www.streetvendor.org
StreetNet International: www.streetnet.org
International Food and Beverage Alliance (IFBA): www.ifbaworld.org

THANK YOU

www.ingramcontent.com/pod-product-compliance
Lightning Source LLC
Chambersburg PA
CBHW070918220526
45467CB00004B/1466